I0965717

to drink coffee with a ghost

to drink coffee with a ghost

amanda lovelace

Andrews McMeel

PUBLISHING®

books by amanda lovelace

the
women are some kind of magic
series:

the princess saves herself in this one (#1)
the witch doesn't burn in this one (#2)
the mermaid's voice returns in this one (#3)

slay those dragons: a journal for writing
your own story

***

the
things that h(a)unt
duology:

to make monsters out of girls (#1)
to drink coffee with a ghost (#2)

this is dedicated
to the one
who loves ketchup
as much as
i do.

trigger warning

child abuse,
eating disorders,
sexual assault,
self-harm,
violence,
cheating,
death,
gore,
blood,
trauma,
grief,
& possibly
more.

remember to practice
self-care before,
during, & after
reading.

contents

when she thinks
i have forgotten her,

every phone
rings off the hook—

every television screen
turns to static—

every faucet
twists on & off—

every clock
strikes three a.m.—

every book
flies off the shelves—

every cabinet
swings wide open—

every stool
turns upside down—

every door
locks & unlocks itself—

every lightbulb
explodes into pieces.

i haven't
forgotten;

there are
just some things

i choose
not to remember.

- *welcome home.*

whenever i think of you, i envision our little white kitchen table. inside the drywall, i imagine years of collected stories & laughter burrowed like chestnuts from stowaway squirrels. my secrets are hidden among them, too—the ones you expertly ignored so you could still look at me & see the perfect daughter who never existed. none of these memories would be complete without our coffee. so i sit down at our little white kitchen table. i pour not one but two cups. i wait & wait & wait even though i know you won't show up to hear what i have to say.

- *communication was never our strong suit.*

ghost mother

lately, it seems like everywhere i look, i only find daughters haunted by something their mothers did to them. we tell each other that we would raise our daughters differently. we do this while wondering if our mothers made the same promises to themselves.

- *ghost-mother.*

you walked
underneath streetlamps
& they flickered
until they died.

you wore
watches on your wrist
& time forever
paused.

you drove
brand-new cars
& they stalled on
the freeway.

you held
my bundled-up body
& i looked up at you like
you were the sun.

- *power is power even if it takes.*

"you were an accident,"
she said.

- *it always sounded like "the thing that*
  ruined everything."

you wanted me to adore you most of all, so you handed me prettily wrapped lies in the hopes that i would hesitate before trusting anyone besides you.

- not even myself.

while i was growing bigger & bigger inside your stomach, you still decided to smoke your cigarettes each & every day. "it was normal back then," you explained to me once. "no one knew how dangerous it was. no one knew it could kill."

- *even if you knew, it wouldn't have changed anything.*

i wonder if anyone would be surprised to find out that i came out of you searching for the scent of smoke, which really just ended up being the smell of you.

- *something toxic.*

the little girl was so desperate to feel loved, to feel like she existed at all, that she took anything she could get, even if it was nothing but a bunch of make-believe.

- *don't accept scraps.*

i watched

a
strange man
punch
a hole
through
our family.

i watched

you
hold his hand
& do nothing
as he pushed
your children
through it.

- *aren't mothers supposed to protect?*

you
had me
rehearse
the tales
that would
protect
you.

- *white lies.*

&
you were
shocked
when i started
telling tales
to protect
myself.

- *red lies.*

relationships fail. people break up. families completely collapse in on themselves, folding up at the spine like a bedtime story finished much too soon. but what those bedtime stories fail to do is prepare us for any of it.

- some lessons we must learn for ourselves.

she was
like a
mother
when
she
should have
just been
my
sister.

- *thank you for your sacrifice.*

she
was busy
hiding
her bruises
while
i was busy
hiding
my tears.

- *we were all each other had.*

your
mother
taught you
to hate your
body,

- *family heirloom.*

so
you
taught me
to hate my
body.

- *family heirloom II.*

it wasn't long
before i realized
i could never be
who you always
wanted me
to be.

- *i tried desperately to be her anyway.*

what
you
told me
after

                you saw

the
thin lines
on
my wrist.

\- *"depression doesn't exist."*

i used to turn to you. with scraped knees.
with paper-cut fingers. with battle wounds
from playground wars. then things changed
& i didn't feel like i could do that anymore,
so i turned to people who knew exactly what
i was going through.

> *help, i cut myself so deep i*
> *think i may have to go to the*
> *emergency room.*

> *help, i haven't eaten in two*
> *days & i'm afraid i'll die if i*
> *don't & also if i do.*

> *help, he touched me & i still*
> *feel his fingers.*

when you found out, you locked me up.
buried the key someplace you forgot
about. you gave my pain a name & it
sounded like *rebellion,* not *depression.* no
one ever bothered to tell you about the sad
type of daughter & you did everything
possible not to see her.

- blindfold.

you did not have a medicine spoon filled with poison. you had no gun. no knife. no ax. no belt. no ready hand. however, the weapon you *did* wield proved to be equally as dangerous.

- *your words.*

if i didn't
lose weight,
you said
i was
disgusting.

- there was never any winning with you.

if i lost
too much weight,
you said
i was
disgusting.

- *there was never any winning with you II.*

your best friend.
your fear.

- *they can be one in the same.*

everything i love, i love because you taught me to. when you decided i was finally old enough, you gave me my first deck of tarot cards for my birthday. you told me, *these aren't magick. not by themselves. they're magick because your hands are the ones holding them.*

- *my high priestess.*

most of the time, the person who hurts you is the person who makes your face light up more than the moon at full brightness. they can even be the person who takes you out for your favorite dessert after you've had an awful day. or the person who teaches you the names of crystals. or the person who shows you which offerings to make faeries to get them on your side.

- *it's not your fault that you trusted them.*

you gave me
this great
escape—
shelves
& shelves
of adventures—
but i used them
to escape
you.

- *books upon books upon books.*

i walk
the thin line
between
nostalgia
& trauma,
never fully
knowing
the difference.

- *maybe there is none.*

if poetry showed me how to bleed without the demand of blood, then why do i keep picking open all my old wounds just to get some red on the page?

- my ledger.

I. a noun.
II. one word.
III. five letters.
IV. two syllables.
V. a shot to the lung.

- *cancer.*

i watched you

throw up from chemo.
deteriorate from radiation.
lose every hair.
grow bedsores.
become unrecognizable.
confuse me for others.
clutch your dusty rosary.
receive last rites.
(twice).

- *going . . . going . . . gone.*

you suffered for so long no one believed it
would ever end.

- *nobody deserves that kind of pain.*

there is a kind of cold you're overcome with when you see your first dead body & it has nothing to do with the temperature outside. you keep that cold with you for the rest of your life. it reminds you to live your life more cautiously. to cherish every autumn sunrise & every smile from a loved one. you never know what you'll be allowed to bring with you into the unknown.

- *what if it's nothing?*

what do we do
with all the things
we need to say
to someone
we'll never see
again?

- *maybe that's why i write.*

the july before you left, it rained every fucking day. everything in your precious garden drowned.

- *how can life be over so quickly?*

ghost daughter

one minute, you were here; the next, you had already gone. now i'm terrified to leave a room without saying goodbye to everyone inside of it first.

- what if they disappear like you did?

i wake up
because
i think
i hear you
calling
my name.

i know it
can't be real
because
you died
without
remembering it.

- *it was just wishful thinking.*

you cannot
have a funeral
for your mother
without also
having a funeral
for yourself.

- it's time to begin the procession.

i wish
i had known
i was never
going to
see you again
because i would have
spent more time
clinging to the good
we did have
instead of
clinging to the bad
i couldn't
change.

- *what eats me alive.*

for months,
i dream that
you aren't
really
dead—

that
they made
some sort
of horrible
mistake

by
declaring
you dead &
turning you
to ash

&
you get to
come back
home
now.

- *it feels more like a nightmare.*

she learned
that dead moms
were not just
a thing that

happened to
characters
in her favorite
fairy tales.

it happened to
girls like her, too,
but the
difference was

there was no
omniscient narrator
to teach her how
to navigate it.

- *the cracked compass.*

"what will she do without a mommy?"
the little girl asked.

- *i still don't know.*

celebrities died. pets died. even distant relatives died. back then, grief seemed so easy, effortless. so meaningful, even hopeful. nowadays, grief is so fucking messy. grief is an off-white coffee mug with fading green rings around the top in the far-left corner of the kitchen cabinet, spider webs filling it to the brim, & no, i can't just throw it away even though you've been gone for years because how would you ever forgive me for that?

- *sometimes there is no meaning.*

i wonder what you would say if you saw me now. you were the one who passed on, but i'm the one who forgot what it was to live. i barely sleep & all the flesh is falling off my bones & my books—all my beloved books— are coated in inches of dust, unread. here i am, somehow managing to be more haunted house than girl.

- *ghost-daughter.*

"i only ever wanted to keep you safe,"
you screamed.

"then why didn't you?"
i cried.

- *lucid.*

remember
back when
we always
stayed up
way too late
watching
our favorite
ghost shows
on tv?

- *now you're the ghost story & i can't bring
  myself to watch those shows anymore.*

without you,
it's lonely.

- *it doesn't have to make sense.*

without you,
it's liberating.

- it doesn't have to make sense II.

i'm afraid i'll be just like you.
i'm afraid i'll be nothing like you.

- *my empress in reverse.*

i used to tell people you were the lorelai to my rory. the ultimate package: not just mother & daughter, but the best of friends. as i grow older, i wonder how many times rory went to bed feeling empty, wishing for a mother, & just that—a mother. for that someone who would tell her what she needed to do when life was just too much to handle without ever expecting anything from her in return.

- chasing emily.

even
the old
coffee-ring
stains
on the tables
at cafés
remind me
of you.

- *you're everywhere & nowhere all at once.*

i tell everyone i can't bake & what i mean to say is that i *won't* bake. before you got really, really sick, you tried to teach me everything you possibly could. even though you were confident that you would beat it, i think you knew you were quickly running out of time & we had to squeeze a lifetime of lessons into a year. now, i can't taste burnt chocolate chip cookies without thinking of you.

- the conjuring.

without you
i'm not
quite sure
who the fuck
i'm supposed
to be.

- *dependent.*

in all
the history
of the world
no one has ever
been able to
teach others
how to fill the hole
a dead parent
leaves.

- *impossibilities.*

i cannot fight my way through these fucking
shadows on my own.

- *no light, no sun.*

i only
find myself
kissing boys
who love
to make
monsters
out of
girls.

- *a guide on how to self-destruct.*

my lovers know i'm bad luck. when they sneak back home, they throw sea salt over their shoulders with one hand as they call their girlfriends with the other. they say, *oh honey, i lost track of time.* they say, *oh sweetheart, i missed you so much.* they say, *oh beautiful, don't worry about her. she's no one. she's nothing at all.*

- they were right.

tell me
you love me
even if
you have to
cross your fingers
behind your back
while you
do it.

- *i don't mind being lied to, baby.*

there
was not
a single kiss
from my
lips
that was
not laced
with
devastation.

- *my lovers in reverse.*

i always believed that if i was able to make them stay, they would make me forget every bad thing that ever happened to me. they always told me that they would rescue me from myself & i was foolish enough to believe them.

- *bittersweet.*

i keep searching for a mother in every woman i meet, but if i'm being honest, i wouldn't even begin to know what it is i'm supposed to be looking for.

- *which parts make up a mother?*

they said to me,

> *you can't be angry at your mother. you*
> *can't be angry at your sick mother. you*
> *can't be angry at your dead mother.*
> *you can't be angry.*

i wanted to take the floor & scream,

> *my trauma doesn't get wiped away*
> *just because it's inconvenient for*
> *you to love someone who was also*
> *capable of causing others pain.*

- hard feelings.

your
comfort
is not
more
important
than
my journey
to
healing.

- i will never live a life of quiet again.

i
remember
hearing
somewhere
that

once
you've heard
your
mother's
voice,

you're
never (*ever*)
able
to forget it
again.

i've
already
started
forgetting
yours.

- i don't want to think about what's next.

people keep asking me if i love you or hate you. the answer has never been as simple as *yes* or *no*. of course i love you, but i hate so much of what you did.

- *tug of war.*

my therapist believes in ghosts & she thinks you might be haunting me. she tells me to wait until the house is completely empty. she tells me to light a candle. she tells me to wish you well but wish you gone. i don't tell her this, but i light no candle. i cast no protective circle. instead, i walk around the house in a towel screaming,

why won't you go?
you can't hold me back.
i'm allowed to move on.
you can't live through me.
let me be happy for once.
leave.
leave.
leave.

- the cleansing.

sun-showers

how do you keep on living after the worst imaginable thing happens to you? there is no easy answer—no steps 1, 2, & 3. i just remember waking up one day & deciding that i would try to remember that even though rainstorms are completely unavoidable, sun-showers exist, too. whenever it feels like your world is crashing down all around you, the sun will always be there to warm you between the wrath of the storm.

- *sun-showers.*

i realize now
you were
never
haunting
me.

- *you were just keeping me company.*

you carried
your demons
& you tried
your best to
shoulder
mine, too.

yours were
just
too heavy
a burden
to take on
the load.

- *with age comes wisdom.*

grief is a funny thing. for years, it made me forget that fairy tales existed. then one day, i remembered. just like that, everything was enchanted mirrors & talking clocks again. from then on, i simply couldn't get my fill of them; it was as if i was learning to read all over again. books became magick in my hands—the same magick you always told me i had. you were right all along: some things don't come alive until we believe in them with our whole hearts.

- *never will i forget again.*

eventually,
the rain just
sounds like
rain—

like
getting comfy
with a
good book

beneath
a pile of cats
while holding
a cup of coffee.

none of it is sad.
not once do i
picture you
beside me.

i'm alone,
& for the first time,
i'm okay with
being alone.

- *because you're never truly alone with
  a book.*

i don't necessarily think you should have to forgive those who have mistreated you in the most life-defining ways. forgiveness is something sacred. however, i would like to think i could forgive you, if given the opportunity. i would like to think you would give me reason to.

- here's hoping.

i can
no longer
focus on
everything
i've lost.

no matter
how many times
i hit replay,
i can't change
anything.

i vow to focus
on whatever else
the universe
has in store
for me.

- *my six of cups reversed.*

to
underestimate
women
is bad enough
by itself,
but
i imagine
anyone
who does
must not know
many sisters.

- *together, we are strong as hell.*

we are exactly the same & yet somehow exactly different. i am the introvert to your extrovert. we both love ketchup on everything we eat. i hate to cry in front of people, whereas you cry tears of fearlessness. we have the same favorite band. whenever one of us feels compelled to crumble, the other distracts the rest of the world while she slowly rebuilds, stone by heavy stone.

- *this has always been the secret to our survival.*

we
have
the same
numb toe.

we
have
the same
lump on our heads.

we
have
the same
roaring laugh.

we
even
have
the same
hard-to-swallow
memories.

- *how could i not love you?*

when i think
of my life
without a sister,
i suddenly
understand
what they mean
when they say
people can die
from broken
hearts.

- *the worst tragedy of all.*

the only way i found relief in this grieving was to plant gravestones everywhere my feet treaded. the first time they leaned in to kiss me, i hesitated. they were far too perfect—far too *alive*—to become a haunted, hunted thing like i was.

- *selfishly, i kissed them anyway.*

my gods,
you shine
so brightly
i can't even
look at you
straight
on.

- *striking.*

"give me space to heal,"
i asked of them.

- *the courage i never felt before.*

"you don't even need to ask,"
they replied.

- *the respect i'd never been shown.*

they do not pretend to deserve me; better yet, they do not even pretend that they can save me. they do not view me as a broken, feathered thing they can mend up if they scoop me into their hands & show me enough attention. in time, they know that i will stretch across the skies again, but not before i'm ready.

- not before i mend my own wing.

for the first time, i will allow myself to believe that the best can & will happen to me, instead of the worst.

- life doesn't have to be a horror show.

they proved
to me
that sometimes—
just sometimes—
people do not
leave.

- my reliable forever.

no one
has to
understand
what we are
as long as
we do.

- *we're the only thing that matters.*

i would carve silly faces
into pumpkins
with you.

- *how i say "i love you."*

i would drink
all the bad coffee
with you.

- *how i say "i love you" II.*

&
i don't think

i would mind
spending

the rest
of our lives

sitting
on the floor,

eating
crappy pizza

on top of
moving boxes

we
never

end up
unpacking.

- *because i would have you.*

they all
want to
know why
i call you
my sun-heart.

- *it's because you cast a shadow nowhere.*

in this story, they do not leave even though things are difficult at times. they are gentler with my heart than any who came before them & any who would dare to come after in the next life. if you want to know what kind of person they are, i should tell you that the first time they took me to the water, we spent the entire time rescuing ladybugs from being pulled out with the current.

- you left me in life-saving hands.

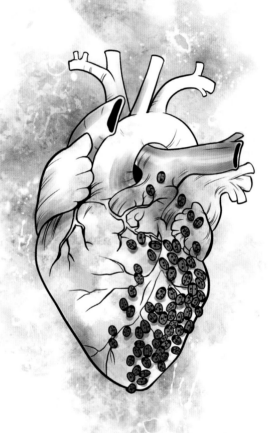

i unlearn
the idea
that
it's normal
to fear
the drive
home
when
they're
the one
i'm driving
home to
at the end
of the
day.

- *no small feat.*

i thought
no one
could know me
without
knowing where
i got my love
for coffee creamer
or halloween,
but they're
doing just
fine.

- *i've always been whole on my own.*

despite her fears, my sister asks me to read her cards. the first thing she asks them is if you regret what you did to us & the card practically flies out. this time, i don't even bother looking up the meaning; no book could possibly understand. it's the definition of defeat. it's regret. it's guilt. it's wishing that you could have fixed what happened while you were still alive to do it. it's knowing that you'll never be able to. it's everything we wanted to hear & somehow— somehow, it's enough & not enough all at the same time.

- *our five of swords.*

i have my own white kitchen table now. it's not little; it's the size of an entire lifetime left to live. it's never a place of fear, judgment, or silencing. at this table, i've shared coffee & quiet truths with my love. at this table, i've shared meals & laughter with friends & family. at this table, i have imagined stories with princesses who save themselves, witches who never burn, & mermaids who remember their voices. no matter what happens, i will never allow my kitchen table to be anything but a place where love & healing thrives.

- the letter i cannot send.

i picked up my entire life & moved into a small apartment by the very stretch of sea you wanted to be your last resting place. i'm not sure why i did it. part of it felt like this was the place i was meant to call my home, & part of it felt like it was the only place i could find you again, like the good doctor who went to find the ghost of his wife in small mountain town, colorado.

i tried to turn my life into fiction & i was surprised when it didn't work. i never found you here—i found your ghost, but not *you*. at least i can say it was a learning experience. i learned that i never should have built the rest of my life around the idea what could have been.

you were never the point to my story. i am.

as i write this, i'm once again surrounded by moving boxes. i didn't want to leave, but i have to. the universe has made its decision without me & it has let me know that this town was never meant for you nor me. in just a few weeks, i'm moving to another town completely unmarked by you or the plans you had for me.

i'm buying my first house & you'll never get to see it, just like you never got to see me graduate from college or meet the love of my life or be there for my wedding. it hurt— all of it—but somehow, i survived it all. i know i can survive the rest, too, since i've done it so many times already.

i'm not helpless.

truth is, i never was.

in the winter when all the trees are bare, i can see the ocean from the front door i call my own now. i search for you out of habit, but i don't see a sign of you anywhere. the cold doesn't feel so cold anymore. it's then i accept that i was always meant to do this on my own.

- *the letter i cannot send II.*

you may or may not know this, but i had an october wedding. i wore a dress in your favorite color (red) & a flower crown in the most beautiful autumn colors. things have gotten much better in the years since you've been gone, but most days, i do not feel even a fraction beautiful. that day, i felt nothing short of a goddess.

looking back, it feels more like a lucid dream than a memory. something ethereal, unearthly. just out of touch.

it sounds old-fashioned, but i let dad give me away. it felt less like an exchange of property & more a moment of, "here she is. she has been through so very much in the little bit of life she has lived so far. i'm the only parent she has left, & i'm trusting you not to give her more pain than she is able to take. no—she is not breakable, but she is human, after all."

despite everything, i have always experienced moments in which i wished you were there beside me to experience it. that day, i didn't have to wish for that. i felt you everywhere. in every cold breeze, in the light between the treetops.

everywhere, i felt an apology for your absence.

even after our angry goodbye, i knew you never left. you just went into hiding. if you're staying because you feel guilty you're missing out on my life, then please let me put your mind to rest: the road to forgiveness may be a long, uneven one that has no true ending, but that doesn't lessen my love for you or my desire to finally see you at peace.

there's no reason for you to be afraid anymore. as frightening as the unknown can be, remember that wherever you may be going next, you will still remain in every facet of my life. we have plenty of time to drink coffee & catch up later.

this is my lit candle.
this is my protective circle.
this is where we finally say "goodbye."

- *the letter i cannot send III.*

when she had almost no friends, she had the tiny globes of light. they trailed behind her everywhere she went, & some nights they burned so brightly she did nothing but toss & turn. one day, the globes burned even brighter—so bright she thought it was time to look into the face of death & smile. when they dimmed again, surrounded was she by people who understand every part of her. she never realized what the lights meant till now: the light was always leading her to them, her found family forged in weirdness & laughter.

& it was so good.

oh my god, it was so good.

- what it feels to belong.
  after iain s. thomas

you
showed me
that blood
is no
competition
for
the
bodies
of water
between
us.

- *long-distance friendships.*

you're so unreal
i don't think
i could have
even known
to manifest
you.

- *the universe marvels at you.*

i'm starting to think that maybe i had the wrong idea about soul mates all along. they won't necessarily be your lover, but they can be. maybe all our lovers are our soul mates. maybe all our friends are, too. our acquaintances, even. do you ever think about the word? soulmate. maybe we should start calling them *soulmeets* instead—souls that were destined to meet & impact each other in the most gentle & unpredictable ways.

- finding new meaning.

sharing the same family tree doesn't often make people stay. find family in the ones who make you laugh uncontrollably. find family in the ones who take your side but also talk you through your wrongdoings. find family in the ones who would hop on a plane & fly across countries the moment you needed them. find family in the ones who rejoice in you, especially when you're unsure of yourself. find the ones who will face the fire with you.

- they're your real family.

hold tightly
to
the ones
who
not only
know you
but
take the time
& energy
to
understand
the intricacies
of your
magic.

- *what's truly important.*

you are not
a disappointment.

you are not
the culmination

of what people
expect of you.

- life is not a pass or fail.

you may
be
a product
of whoever
raised you,

- *you choose*

but you
belong
to nobody
except
yourself.

- *your own future.*

the
ways
in which
they
suffer
themselves
is not
an excuse
to
make you
suffer
in
return.

- let me get "controversial" for a moment II.

sometimes—
sometimes,
it's the loss
of someone
that makes you
complete.

- *life is funny like that.*

grief will
never truly be
done with you.

when
you're ready,
take it in your hands

like a paintbrush.
like a charcoal.
like a pen.

turn it
into a thing that
could hang in museums.

- *masterpiece.*

most hauntings can be explained away by normal, everyday occurrences—old water pipes, a crumbling foundation, a family of mice scurrying around in the attic. other times, we're the ones haunting ourselves. give your ghost a voice. open up all the doors & windows. let the world hear you. let them carry the hurt your shoulders can no longer bear to hold.

- only then will you be finally be free.

when the veil between the living & the departed is thinnest every year, i come to you for guidance. this year, i pull the reaper. if i didn't know any better, i would be terrified, but i feel nothing but peace. after all, the reaper rarely actually comes with warnings of death or catastrophe. this year, i know he comes in place of you. you tell me it's time to stop taking these walks through the past & to start making room for the future. when life gives us new beginnings, we need to take them, because there are never enough of them.

- *your death in reverse.*

"i hope you can find it
in your heart to be proud

of the woman i have become
in spite of you."

- *the princess saves herself in this one*

acknowledgments

this book—no, this *series*—is what it is because of your lovely artwork, *munise sertel*. thank you so much for working with me again!

my sister, *courtney*, helped me with this book more than she will ever realize. thank you for encouraging me to tell this story, even when it got messy & even a little bit scary at times. you know what? i think i might love you *more* than ketchup.

of course, a thousand thank-yous to my ever-supportive *dad* & *stepmom*. for every book you buy. for every event you go to. for every facebook post you share. for every cat picture sent. your support will always mean the world to me.

without my spouse, *cyrus parker*, i probably would have quit this writing thing a long time ago. many thanks for keeping me inspired & with coffee. <3 my critique partner, the extremely lovely *christine day*, is another reason why i stay motivated. whenever i fear for the worst, you bring me back to reality & help me get my shit together. for that, i will always be grateful. here's to our second series together & to (hopefully) many more to come! *clink*

trista mateer, aka peaches—"thank you" will never be enough to account for just how much you helped with this book, but thank you anyway for making it a much less traumatic experience than it would have been. i'm pretty sure you "get" my books more than i do!

endless gratitude to my faithful beta reader, *mira kennedy*. where would i be today without your grammar corrections? nowhere, that's where. thank you for sticking around.

thank you to *nikita (fucking) gill* for keeping me empowered enough to keep going in all aspects of my life, but especially when it comes to my writing. i adore you, my queen. my sister. my everything. i want to be you when i grow up.

to my editor, *patty rice*, as well as the rest of my team at andrews mcmeel publishing: thank you for having faith in me & for making this weird little book series possible in the first place!

lastly, thank *you*, whether you've been supporting my work since book one, or you just started now. this journey wouldn't be worth it without you.

about the author

having grown up a word-devourer & avid fairy tale lover, it was only natural that amanda lovelace began writing books of her own. so she did. when she isn't reading or writing, she can be found waiting for pumpkin spice coffee to come back into season & binge-watching *gilmore girls.* (before you ask: team jess all the way.) the lifelong poetess & storyteller currently lives in new jersey with her spouse, their ragdolls, & a combined book collection so large it will soon need its own home. she is a two-time winner of the goodreads choice award for best poetry as well as a *usa today* & *publishers weekly* bestseller.

index

Andrews McMeel Publishing
a division of Andrews McMeel Universal
1130 Walnut Street, Kansas City, Missouri 64106

www.andrewsmcmeel.com

19 20 21 22 23 SDB 10 9 8 7 6 5 4 3 2 1

ISBN: 978-1-4494-9427-8

Library of Congress Control Number: 2019938136

Illustrations by Munise Sertel

Editor: Patty Rice
Designer/Art Director: Julie Barnes
Production Editor: Dave Shaw
Production Manager: Cliff Koehler

ATTENTION: SCHOOLS AND BUSINESSES
Andrews McMeel books are available at quantity discounts
with bulk purchase for educational, business, or sales
promotional use. For information, please e-mail the
Andrews McMeel Publishing Special Sales Department:
specialsales@amuniversal.com.